THE POETRY OF GALLIUM

The Poetry of Gallium

Walter the Educator™

SKB

Silent King Books a WhichHead Imprint

Copyright © 2023 by Walter the Educator™

All rights reserved. No part of this book may be reproduced in any manner whatsoever without written permission except in the case of brief quotations embodied in critical articles and reviews.

First Printing, 2023

Disclaimer
This book is a literary work; poems are not about specific persons, locations, situations, and/or circumstances unless mentioned in a historical context. This book is for entertainment and informational purposes only. The author and publisher offer this information without warranties expressed or implied. No matter the grounds, neither the author nor the publisher will be accountable for any losses, injuries, or other damages caused by the reader's use of this book. The use of this book acknowledges an understanding and acceptance of this disclaimer.

"Earning a degree in chemistry changed my life!"
- Walter the Educator

dedicated to all the chemistry lovers, like myself, across the world

CONTENTS

Dedication v

Why I Created This Book? 1

One - Oh, Gallium 2

Two - Adapt And Transform 4

Three - Liquid Metal 6

Four - Symbol Of Allure 8

Five - Every Transformation 10

Six - Captivating Sight 12

Seven - Truly Unique 14

Eight - Shifting Forms 16

Nine - Endless Exploration 18

Ten - Wondrous Star 20

Eleven - Work Of Art 22

Twelve - Gallium, The Enigma 24

Thirteen - Forever To Adorn	. . . .	26
Fourteen - Symbol Ga	. . . .	28
Fifteen - Open Mind	. . . .	30
Sixteen - Element Of Dreams	. . . .	32
Seventeen - Unique Metal	. . . .	34
Eighteen - Infinite Guise	. . . .	36
Nineteen - Partner To Science	. . . .	38
Twenty - Tale To Tell	. . . .	40
Twenty-One - 31	. . . .	42
Twenty-Two - Marvel Divine	. . . .	44
Twenty-Three - So Rare	. . . .	46
Twenty-Four - Day By Day	. . . .	48
Twenty-Five - Crystal Clear	. . . .	50
Twenty-Six - Force To Reckon	. . . .	52
Twenty-Seven - Cosmic Scheme	. . . . . .	54
Twenty-Eight - Mesmerizing Element	. . . . .	56
Twenty-Nine - Silently Persists	. . . .	58
Thirty - Moonlit Wine	. . . .	60
Thirty-One - Lasers And LEDs	. . . .	62
Thirty-Two - Whispers In The Air	. . . . . .	64

Thirty-Three - Enchanting Us All 66

Thirty-Four - Gallium's Grace 68

Thirty-Five - Intricate Hand 70

Thirty-Six - Hidden Gem 72

About The Author 74

WHY I CREATED THIS BOOK?

Creating a poetry book about the chemical element of Gallium was a unique and fascinating endeavor. Gallium, with its atomic number 31 and symbol Ga, possesses several interesting properties and characteristics that can be explored through the medium of poetry. By delving into its history, discovery, uses, and physical properties, this poetry book can provide a creative and artistic perspective on Gallium. Through the power of words and imagery, this book can capture the essence of this element, its significance in various fields, and its impact on the world. It can also serve as an educational tool, making science more accessible and engaging for readers.

ONE

OH, GALLIUM

In the realm of elements, hidden in plain sight,
Lies a silver beauty, Gallium's might.
A metal so rare, a sight to behold,
Its secrets and wonders, yet to be told.

    With a melting point low, like secrets untold,
Gallium dances, as it turns into gold.
A trickster it plays, in the palm of your hand,
A solid, a liquid, a marvel so grand.

    Beneath the moon's glow, it shimmers and gleams,
A liquid metal, defying all dreams.
With a touch of warmth, it melts with delight,
Like a lover's caress, on a summer's night.

    Its magic unfolds, when mixed with alloys,
Creating strength, with its metallic joys.

A catalyst it stands, in chemical lore,
Igniting reactions, forevermore.
    Gallium, the element, so pure and refined,
A symbol of progress, a treasure designed.
In science and art, its presence is felt,
A silent companion, in all that is dealt.
    Oh, Gallium, embrace us with your grace,
Guide us through mysteries, we long to embrace.
A metal so rare, yet so endlessly vast,
Gallium, forever, in our hearts it will last.

TWO

ADAPT AND TRANSFORM

In the realm of elements, a secret lies concealed,
A metal rare and precious, with powers unrevealed.
Gallium, they call it, a mystery in disguise,
Its gleaming silver beauty, a wonder to behold with eyes.

Born from the earth's crust, in hidden depths it hides,
A silent observer, where alchemy collides.
Its melting point is low, a mere embrace of heat,
It turns from solid to liquid, a transformation so fleet.

Oh, Gallium, your magic lies in your fluid state,
Like quicksilver, you dance, defying the hands of fate.
You slip through fingers, a playful liquid stream,
A metal with the soul of a dream.

In laboratories, you find your purpose and use,
A catalyst of change, a chemical muse.
You aid in the creation of mirrors so clear,
Reflecting the world, both far and near.

But beyond the confines of science and art,
Gallium, you touch the depths of the heart.
For in your essence, a lesson we learn,
To adapt and transform, to grow and discern.

So, let us celebrate this element rare,
A symbol of resilience, beyond compare.
Gallium, you inspire, with your fluid grace,
A reminder that life is a constant embrace.

In the alchemy of existence, let us strive,
To be like Gallium, adaptable and alive.

THREE

LIQUID METAL

In the depths of the periodic table's realm,
Where elements dance and atoms overwhelm,
There lies a metal, so silvery and bright,
Gallium, a marvel with captivating might.

Born from the Earth, in mines deep below,
Gallium, a treasure, its secrets to bestow,
A liquid metal, defying solid state,
Its properties, peculiar and innate.

At room temperature, it remains fluid,
A shimmering pool, with a touch so eluded,
Its molten essence, a metallic delight,
Captivating hearts with its ethereal light.

Oh, Gallium, your beauty lies within,
A chameleon, adapting with a graceful spin,
In alloys you blend, to enhance and endure,
A versatile companion, steadfast and pure.

From semiconductors to mirrors so clear,
Gallium, you conquer, dispelling all fear,
With gall and gallium arsenide's might,
You revolutionize technology's flight.

But beyond the confines of science's embrace,
Gallium, you leave an indelible trace,
In the hearts of dreamers, who seek to explore,
The wonders of elements, forevermore.

So let us marvel at Gallium's allure,
A liquid metal, so enchantingly pure,
For in its essence, we find a tale,
Of elements dancing, a cosmic unveil.

FOUR

SYMBOL OF ALLURE

In the depths of the periodic table's embrace,
Lies a shimmering secret, a Gallium grace.
A metal so alluring, yet humble and rare,
Shining with brilliance, beyond compare.

    Oh, Gallium, your beauty knows no bounds,
A liquid at ease, in the warmth it surrounds.
Mercurial in nature, you dance with delight,
Melting in my palm, like a dream taking flight.

    A trickster element, with a mischievous smile,
You defy expectations, in your liquid-style.
Your low melting point, a secret to behold,
As you slip through my fingers, so gentle and bold.

    Oh, Gallium, you enchant with your silvery sheen,
A metal that defies the rigid routine.

A chemist's delight, a conductor of heat,
A catalyst, a partner, in reactions so sweet.
    From lightbulbs to mirrors, you play your role,
A versatile element, with secrets untold.
In alloys and semiconductors, you find your place,
Contributing to progress, with grace and embrace.
    Oh, Gallium, you are a mystery, so rare,
A symbol of wonder, beyond compare.
As I ponder your essence, I can't help but see,
The magic that lies in your atomic decree.
    So, let us celebrate your ethereal fame,
Gallium, the element, forever shall claim,
A place in our hearts, a symbol of allure,
A reminder of beauty, in nature so pure.

FIVE

EVERY TRANSFORMATION

In a realm of metals, rare and fine,
Where elements dance in a cosmic design,
There lies a treasure, gallium its name,
A tale of marvel, a story to proclaim.

A liquid metal, its beauty untold,
With a silver sheen, so precious, so bold,
Atop the periodic table, it takes its place,
An enigma of nature, with an elegant grace.

Its melting point, a mere breath away,
A flicker of heat, and it starts to sway,
From solid to liquid, it transforms with ease,
Defying expectations, as if to tease.

Its touch, oh so gentle, on fingertips light,
A cool sensation, a soothing delight,

With magical powers, it dances on skin,
Caressing the senses, a whisper so thin.

Yet gallium, in secret, holds a power untamed,
When blended with others, its nature is reclaimed,
An alloy companion, creating bonds so strong,
Forging connections, where once there was none.

A catalyst of change, in every reaction,
Unifying elements, with an unseen attraction,
Gallium, a symbol of adaptability and grace,
An element of wonder, in this vast cosmic space.

So let us celebrate, this marvel of the earth,
A liquid metal, of infinite worth,
Gallium, our muse, our poetic inspiration,
A symbol of potential, in every transformation.

SIX

CAPTIVATING SIGHT

In the realm of elements, gallium shines,
A metal with a spirit, rare and fine.
Born from the earth, its beauty untold,
A tale of mystery, yet to unfold.

Liquid silver, it dances with delight,
At melting point, a captivating sight.
From solid to liquid, a graceful transition,
Gallium's essence, a mystical rendition.

An alchemist's dream, it does inspire,
With properties that spark the fire.
Low boiling point, it defies the norm,
Gallium, a rebel in its own form.

In the laboratory, it finds its place,
An element that leaves no trace.

A catalyst, it speeds reactions anew,
Gallium, the magician, changing the view.
    But beyond the lab, its wonders extend,
For gallium is a loyal friend.
With gallium arsenide, it lights up our screens,
A messenger of technology's dreams.
    Oh gallium, you stand apart,
A metal that captures the heart.
In your presence, magic takes flight,
An element that ignites pure delight.

SEVEN

TRULY UNIQUE

Gallium, a metal that's liquid at room temperature,
A phenomenon that defies our imagination's stature.
It's unique, it's rare, and it's fascinating to see,
How a metal can be fluid and yet so free.
    Its melting point is just above thirty degrees,
And its properties are nothing short of a tease.
It's soft and malleable, yet strong and tough,
A metal that can do things that others can't enough.
    Gallium, you're a mystery that we can't quite solve,
A metal that's elusive and we can't quite evolve.
You're used in semiconductors, LEDs, and more,
A wonder metal that we just can't ignore.
    Your atomic number is thirty-one,
And your atomic weight is just above sixty-one.

You're a metal that's not quite like the rest,
A unique element that's simply the best.
    So here's to Gallium, a metal that's so rare,
A wonder that we all can't help but stare.
You're a chemical element that's truly unique,
And we can't wait to see what you'll achieve.

EIGHT

SHIFTING FORMS

In the depths of science's realm,
Where elements and secrets dwell,
There lies a metal, rare and bright,
A gallant gallium, shining with might.
    Born from the earth's hidden core,
A liquid silver, evermore,
It dances in the furnace's heat,
With melting point so low, yet sweet.
    Gallium, a metal with a soul,
Its properties, a wondrous goal,
A chameleon, shifting forms,
Adapting to the world's demands.
    A gallium heart, pure and true,
It binds with others, strong and new,

Alloys forged in fiery embrace,
Creating strength, defying space.

    From semiconductors to mirrors' delight,
Gallium's touch brings forth the light,
A catalyst for progress and change,
Innovation's ally, never estranged.

    A liquid metal, an enigma in disguise,
Flowing through the veins of science's prize,
With gallium's touch, we reach the stars,
Unveiling mysteries from afar.

    Oh gallium, element divine,
A symbol of possibilities, oh so fine,
In your essence, we find endless grace,
A testament to chemistry's embrace.

    So let us celebrate this metal rare,
With gallium's glow, we'll all share,
A tribute to the wonders it imparts,
Gallium, forever etched in our hearts.

NINE

ENDLESS EXPLORATION

In a realm where metals dance and play,
In the depths of the periodic array,
There lies an element, shining bright,
Gallium, a beauty, casting its light.

With a silver hue, so elegant and rare,
Gallium, the element beyond compare,
Its melting point, a mystery untold,
As it turns from solid to liquid, bold.

At room temperature, solid and still,
But hold it in your hands, and feel the thrill,
For Gallium, it softly begins to flow,
A liquid metal, a mesmerizing show.

It dances with grace, defying the norms,
A shape-shifting marvel, as it transforms,

From a solid, rigid and strong,
To a liquid, fluid and moving along.

    Gallium, the element that defies the rules,
A rebel among metals, breaking the tools,
It finds its place in the heart of the lab,
Where scientists marvel, curious and fab.

    Oh, Gallium, you challenge our minds,
With properties unique, rare to find,
You teach us that in the realm of science,
There's always room for delightful defiance.

    So let us celebrate this wondrous element,
With its mysteries and wonders, so significant,
Gallium, a symbol of endless exploration,
In the realm of chemistry, a true revelation.

TEN

WONDROUS STAR

In the depths of science's realm,
A story of Gallium unfolds,
A metal rare, a tale to tell,
Of secrets hidden within its hold.

    A shimmering liquid, silver hue,
Gallium dances with liquid grace,
Its melting point, a marvel true,
A touch of warmth, it starts to embrace.

    From bismuth's womb, it takes its birth,
A silent rebel, it breaks the mold,
Defying structure, it finds its worth,
A unique element, brave and bold.

    Its atoms, like a symphony,
Arrange in patterns, fluid and free,

A crystalline dance, a sight to see,
In every molecule, a harmony.

Gallium, a magician's delight,
A metal that defies the night,
It melts and molds, with gentle might,
A chameleon, shifting in plain sight.

In circuits and screens, it finds its place,
An ally to technology's haste,
A conductor of electrons' race,
Gallium, the element of embrace.

Oh, Gallium, you wondrous star,
A substance that defies the norm,
With every property you possess,
You leave us in awe and transform.

ELEVEN

WORK OF ART

In the depths of science's realm, a metal gleams,
A liquid beauty, gallium it seems.
A dance of atoms, fluid and free,
An element of wonder, a marvel to see.

    Silvery and soft, it defies the norm,
Melting in your hand with a gentle warmth.
Lowly upon the periodic table it lies,
Yet its properties hold a grand surprise.

    At room's embrace, it remains a solid,
But a gentle touch turns it quite liquid.
A mesmerizing transformation, a magical shift,
Gallium's secret, a scientist's gift.

    Its liquid allure, a trickster's delight,
Mischief it plays, in darkness or light.

A metal, yet not, a liquid, but sure,
Gallium dances, forever obscure.

In the world of alloys, it finds its place,
Strengthening bonds with its molecular grace.
With aluminum, it forms a sturdy bond,
Creating strength, where it was once fond.

Gallium, the chameleon, forever changing,
Adapting, shifting, rearranging.
An element unique, a marvel of its own,
A liquid metal, gallium has grown.

So let us marvel at this liquid's grace,
For gallium's charm, we must embrace.
In the realm of chemistry, it stands apart,
Gallium, a liquid metal, a work of art.

TWELVE

GALLIUM, THE ENIGMA

In the realm of elements, a mystic tale unfolds,
Of a metal so rare, its beauty yet untold.
Gallium, the enigma, with a lustrous silver hue,
An alchemical marvel, captivating and true.

Born from Earth's deep embrace, it emerges with grace,
A symbol, Ga, in the periodic table's embrace.
Atomic number 31, its secrets it conceals,
A shining star among the metals it reveals.

With a melting point low, it defies the norm,
A touch of warmth, and it transforms its form.
From solid to liquid, a mesmerizing dance,
Gallium's fluidity, a symbol of chance.

In laboratories, it finds its purpose and might,

As a catalyst, it sparks reactions, shining bright.
Its alloys, strong and resilient, stand the test of time,
A testament to gallium's strength, truly sublime.

In the world of technology, it finds its domain,
Powering devices with an electric refrain.
From semiconductors to LEDs, its magic unfurls,
Gallium's innovation, in the modern world.

Yet, beyond its science, gallium holds a story,
Of dreams and aspirations, of boundless glory.
A symbol of exploration, a pioneer's call,
Gallium, the element, inspiring one and all.

So let us raise a toast to gallium's grandeur,
A metal that defies limits, a constant adventurer.
In the tapestry of elements, it shines with grace,
Gallium, the enigma, leaving its trace.

THIRTEEN

FOREVER TO ADORN

In the realm of elements, a marvel is found,
Gallium, a metal, so enchanting, renowned.
With a lustrous sheen, like a lunar glow,
It dances with grace, casting an ethereal show.

Beneath the moon's gaze, it begins to melt,
A secret it holds, as its story is felt.
For this metal, so daring, defies common laws,
At a mere touch, it transforms without pause.

From solid to liquid, like a magician's spell,
Gallium bewitches, and its secrets it tells.
In the palm of your hand, it flows like a stream,
A transient beauty, a vision, a dream.

Its low melting point, a curious trait,
Makes it rare, and oh-so-elate.

In thermometers, it measures with grace,
The rise and fall of temperatures' embrace.
   But beyond the lab, in the world outside,
Gallium whispers, in nature it hides.
An ally to technology, it plays a key role,
In semiconductors, it binds us, heart and soul.
   Gallium, an element both rare and fine,
In its elegance, a tale to intertwine.
A metal that dances, defying the norm,
In its mystic allure, forever to adorn.

FOURTEEN

SYMBOL GA

In the realm of elements, a secret lies untold,
A metal called Gallium, with mysteries to unfold.
Symbol Ga, atomic number 31, it stands,
A captivating substance, crafted by nature's hands.

    Gallium, oh Gallium, a liquid silver hue,
Melting in warm hands, defying what we knew.
Low melting point, a whimsical trait it bears,
Transforming solid to liquid, catching us unawares.

    In laboratories, it dances with delight,
Reacting with other elements, a chemical fight.
Its oxides and alloys, a scientist's domain,
Unveiling its potential, a captivating refrain.

    Gallium, oh Gallium, a conductor of sound,
In sonic devices, its magic can be found.

From speakers to microphones, it lends its grace,
Creating harmonies, filling every space.

Yet in the cosmos vast, it has a cosmic role,
For gallium's presence, the stars do extol.
From distant galaxies to celestial spheres,
Its essence permeates, transcending all frontiers.

Gallium, oh Gallium, an enigma in disguise,
A marvel of creation, hidden from our eyes.
In its essence lies a story, waiting to be told,
A testament to nature's wonders, more valuable than gold.

So let us gaze upon this element with awe,
For Gallium's beauty, we can't ignore.
In its shimmering brilliance, we find our delight,
A testament to the wonders of science's might.

FIFTEEN

OPEN MIND

In the realm of elements, Gallium is rare,
A shimmering beauty, beyond compare.
With atomic number thirty-one,
It dances in the light, a radiant sun.

Its silvery hue, like liquid moon,
Melting in my palm, a mystical boon.
A metal so curious, it defies the norm,
Gallium, the alchemist's transforming storm.

At room temperature, it remains solid,
But heat it gently, watch it turn fluid.
A metal with secrets, a shape-shifting trick,
Defying expectations, it's a wondrous mix.

In the confines of science, it finds its place,
But in art and wonder, it leaves a trace.
For Gallium, dear element, holds the key,
To unlock creativity, wild and free.

With a touch of Gallium, a world unfolds,
Of endless possibilities, untold.
From liquid sculptures to mirrors so clear,
It awakens imagination, never to disappear.

Oh, Gallium, you enchanting soul,
In laboratories, your stories unfold.
A metal with mysteries, so beautifully strange,
In your atomic dance, the world rearranges.

So let us celebrate this element rare,
Gallium, the alchemist's captivating affair.
For in its essence, a lesson we find,
To embrace transformation, with an open mind.

SIXTEEN

ELEMENT OF DREAMS

In the land of chemistry, a hidden treasure lies,
A metal of silver, with a mesmerizing guise.
Gallium, they call it, a beauty to behold,
A tale untold, a story yet to be told.

Born from the Earth's crust, in minerals it hides,
A secret kept away, like the moon's gentle tides.
Low melting point, it trickles like a stream,
Liquid silver dreams, in the alchemist's scheme.

An enigma, this element, oh, so rare,
Its presence found in traces, a shimmering affair.
In the shadows it dances, elusive and sly,
A tantalizing mystery, caught by no one's eye.

Gallium, oh gallium, you defy the norm,
With your eccentricities, a scientist's swarm.

You merge with ease, like a chameleon's art,
A metal that melts, a paradox at heart.

A friend to the mirrors that reflect our face,
You coat them with brilliance, with ethereal grace.
In semiconductors, you pave the way,
Enabling technology to flourish, day by day.

Oh gallium, your wonders never cease,
A silent presence, bringing progress and peace.
In this vast universe, where elements collide,
You stand out, gallium, with unabashed pride.

So let us raise a toast, to gallium's might,
A gift from nature, shining ever so bright.
In the realm of chemistry, you reign supreme,
Gallium, the element of dreams.

SEVENTEEN

UNIQUE METAL

In the realm of elements, Gallium resides,
A metal so unique, where its nature hides.
With a lustrous silver hue, it gleams and shines,
A beauty that captivates, a secret it defines.

Born from the Earth, in ores it does rest,
A treasure buried deep, by nature's behest.
Its atomic number, thirty-one it takes,
A symbol Ga, a name that never breaks.

Lowly melting point, a curious trait,
At the touch of warmth, it yields to its fate.
Liquid silver droplets, dancing with glee,
Defying the norm, in a liquid state it be.

Oh, Gallium, a chameleon of the lab,
An alchemist's dream, a magician's fab.
Its metallic touch, a trickster's delight,
Unleashing its magic, with a mischievous sprite.

In semiconductors, it finds its domain,
Powering devices, a technological reign.
Transistors and lasers, it faithfully serves,
Pushing boundaries, as innovation curves.

Yet, beyond the lab, Gallium holds more,
In medicine's realm, it opens new doors.
A radioactive tracer, it guides the way,
Illuminating pathways, where diseases may stray.

Gallium, oh Gallium, a marvel you are,
A silent protagonist, a shining star.
In the world of elements, you stand tall,
Unveiling your secrets, captivating all.

So let us celebrate, this element grand,
With its mysteries and wonders, we'll forever stand.
Gallium, the enigma, we'll forever adore,
A unique metal, forevermore.

EIGHTEEN

INFINITE GUISE

In the realm of elements, where secrets lie,
A shimmering metal, Gallium does imply.
With atomic number thirty-one, it resides,
A mystical substance that effortlessly glides.

Born from the Earth's bosom, a curious find,
Gallium's beauty, a rare sight to unwind.
Its silvery luster, a captivating sheen,
Unveiling mysteries, yet to be seen.

At room temperature, it defies common laws,
A solid, yet liquid, with a hidden cause.
With gentle touch, it melts in your hand,
Like a mystical potion from an enchanted land.

In laboratories, it dances with delight,
Revealing its tricks, both day and night.

A conductor of heat, a conductor of sound,
Gallium, an element that truly astounds.

From gadgets to mirrors, it lends its grace,
In semiconductors, it finds its rightful place.
An ally to technology, it helps us advance,
Gallium, a catalyst for innovation's dance.

Oh, Gallium, a marvel of the periodic table,
Your magic and allure forever enable.
A symbol of progress, a symbol of change,
In your presence, our world will rearrange.

So let us celebrate this fascinating gem,
Gallium, the element that never condemns.
In its essence, a story of wonder and surprise,
A testament to nature's infinite guise.

NINETEEN

PARTNER TO SCIENCE

In the realm where metals dance and sing,
There lies a beauty, a precious thing.
Gallium, the element, so unique and rare,
With its shimmering grace, beyond compare.

    A silvery liquid, it defies the norm,
Melting in hands, like a whispering storm.
Its low melting point, a magical spell,
Transforming to liquid, where others dwell.

    Gallium, the trickster, a shape-shifting wisp,
Playing hide and seek, a playful twist.
From solid to liquid, it bends the rules,
A chameleon element, breaking the tools.

    In the lab, it aids, a catalyst true,
Unleashing reactions, with flair and hue.

A partner to science, a wizard's wand,
Unraveling secrets, beyond the beyond.
 But in nature's realm, it's a rare sight,
Hiding in traces, without a light.
A secret guardian, a hidden gem,
In the depths of Earth, a precious stem.
 Gallium, oh gallium, mysterious and rare,
With your liquid allure, beyond compare.
A symbol of magic, in the periodic tome,
Forever enchanting, in the alchemist's home.

TWENTY

TALE TO TELL

In a realm unseen, where secrets reside,
Lies a metal hidden, where wonders abide.
Gallium, they call it, a whisper in the air,
A mystic element, beyond compare.

Liquid silver it appears, in a spectral dance,
Defying the norms, defying all chance.
Melting with gentle touch, in your palm it gleams,
A trickster in disguise, a creator of dreams.

From deep within the earth, it emerges with might,
A beacon of science, a symbol of light.
Its atomic number, thirty-one it claims,
A symbol of transformation, where magic flames.

In alloys it finds solace, a loyal friend,
Uniting with others, its journey won't end.
With aluminum, it forms a bond so strong,
A union of strength, where they both belong.

But beware the gallium, for it holds a surprise,
A mischief-maker, a trickster in disguise.
It creeps in the circuits, where electronics dwell,
Causing havoc and chaos, a tale to tell.

Oh gallium, enigmatic and rare,
Unveiling your secrets, we're caught in your snare.
A symbol of transformation, a liquid delight,
You captivate our minds, both day and night.

TWENTY-ONE

31

In the depths of science's realm, a metal gleams,
A treasure hidden, Gallium by name it deems.
With atomic number 31, it sits,
A secret whispered by the periodic beats.

Molten magic, its melting point so low,
A touch of warmth, and it begins to flow.
From solid to liquid, a mesmerizing dance,
Gallium, the shape-shifting beauty, enchants.

A metal so soft, it yields without a fight,
A touch from fingers, it surrenders to the light.
A gallant element, gallium shines bright,
A chameleon in nature, changing form with delight.

Beneath the crimson sunset's gentle glow,
Gallium's allure, like dreams, begins to grow.

Its silvery luster reflects the moon's embrace,
A shimmering mirage, an element of grace.
    In laboratories, it finds its place,
A catalyst for progress, a key to embrace.
From semiconductors to LED's glow,
Gallium's significance continues to show.
    Oh, gallant gallium, in science's grand design,
You captivate our minds, like stars that align.
A metal with secrets, a mystery untold,
Gallium, forever an element to behold.

TWENTY-TWO

MARVEL DIVINE

In the realm where metals dance and sing,
A beauty hides, an ethereal thing.
Gallium, a whisper on the periodic chart,
A secret revealed, a work of art.

Liquid silver, with a mystic gleam,
A metal that defies the norm it seems.
At room's embrace, you softly melt,
A shimmering pool, where wonders are dealt.

Oh, Gallium, your nature is rare,
Defying convention, with flair and flair.
Low melting point, a tantalizing trait,
You mock the rules, as you radiate.

In alloys, you bring strength and might,
With titanium, you create a dazzling light.

A conductor of heat, so pure and true,
Gallium, oh Gallium, we cherish you.
   But beware, for you hold a trick up your sleeve,
A gleeful prankster, ready to deceive.
With a touch of warmth, you turn solid again,
Playful Gallium, our delightful friend.
   So here's to you, Gallium, a marvel divine,
A metal that defies the boundaries of time.
In your liquid form or your solid state,
You captivate us, with your enigmatic fate.

TWENTY-THREE

SO RARE

Gleaming Gallium, oh how you shine,
A metal that's liquid, yet so divine,
Your silvery surface reflects the light,
A sight to behold, such a beautiful sight.

You melt in my palms, a fascinating feat,
A low melting point, so unique and sweet,
Your density low, your viscosity high,
Your properties so strange, oh my oh my.

You're used in semiconductors, and LEDs,
In mirrors and even for cancer therapies,
You're a catalyst, a crucial part,
In the world of chemistry, you play a major part.

Gallium, oh Gallium, how you amaze,
With your properties and your strange ways,
A metal that's liquid, yet so strong,
We sing your praises, all day long.

So here's to you, Gallium, oh how you shine,
A metal so unique, so rare and divine,
We'll always cherish, your strange allure,
Gallium, oh Gallium, forever more.

TWENTY-FOUR

DAY BY DAY

In the realm of elements, a beauty lies,
A metal rare, with a gleaming guise,
Gallium, oh Gallium, a marvel unknown,
A liquid treasure, in a world of its own.

Born from the earth, a humble birth,
Silent and unassuming, its intrinsic worth,
A silver drop, with a touch of grace,
Melting in warmth, a delicate embrace.

Alchemist's dream, this enigmatic prize,
Its secrets concealed, behind those eyes,
Soft as a whisper, yet strong as steel,
Gallium, oh Gallium, a mystery surreal.

It dances with light, a shimmering dance,
Defying the rules, in a cosmic trance,

With low melting point, it defies the norm,
Transforming from solid to liquid, in its form.

A conductor of electricity, it plays its part,
In circuits and wires, it ignites the spark,
A catalyst of change, in the chemical realm,
Gallium, oh Gallium, an elemental helm.

In the depths of science, it finds its way,
A catalyst for knowledge, day by day,
Unveiling the secrets, it holds within,
Gallium, oh Gallium, a tale to begin.

So let us marvel at this element rare,
A liquid metal, beyond compare,
Gallium, oh Gallium, a wonder untold,
In the vast universe, its story unfolds.

TWENTY-FIVE

CRYSTAL CLEAR

In a realm where elements dance,
Gallium, a shimmering trance.
A liquid metal, enigmatic and rare,
With secrets hidden in its molecular lair.

A silver tide, it weaves and glides,
Defying the laws that nature provides.
At room's embrace, it remains at ease,
A liquid jewel, the eye can't appease.

In the alchemist's hands, it takes its form,
A shape-shifter, in flux, a chemical storm.
From solid to liquid, a whimsical dance,
Gallium's allure, a beguiling chance.

Its melting point, a mere breath away,
A touch, a warmth, and it begins to sway.

A metal that melts in the palm of your hand,
A surreal sensation, too grand to withstand.
   Beyond the lab, its wonders unfold,
In semiconductors, a story untold.
With gallium arsenide, a new frontier,
Advancing technology, crystal clear.
   From lasers to solar cells, it finds its place,
Empowering progress with each embrace.
Gallium, a catalyst for innovation's call,
A testament to science's rise and fall.
   So, let us marvel at this element's might,
A liquid metal, shining so bright.
Gallium, the enigma we can't comprehend,
A symbol of curiosity, that will never end.

TWENTY-SIX

FORCE TO RECKON

In the realm of elements, behold Gallium's grace,
A silver treasure with a mystifying embrace.
Born from Earth's depths, where secrets lie,
Gallium, the enigma, catches the eye.

With a melting point so low, a mere touch will do,
Transforming solid to liquid, and defying what we knew.
Like a chameleon, it changes its form,
Adapting to heat, a mesmerizing swarm.

Oh, Gallium, you dance with the flames,
A liquid metal, defying all claims.
With a shimmering sheen, like moonlit tears,
You captivate hearts, dispelling all fears.

In laboratories, your secrets unfold,
Revealing your uses, both new and old.

From semiconductors to LEDs so bright,
Gallium, you illuminate the night.

In mirrors and lenses, you lend a hand,
Reflecting light, a spectacle so grand.
With gallium arsenide, you pave the way,
For faster technology, where dreams hold sway.

Oh, Gallium, you're a marvel indeed,
A chemical element, fulfilling our need.
With your unique properties, you inspire,
Pushing boundaries higher and higher.

In the realm of elements, you stand apart,
Gallium, the alchemist's mysterious art.
A symbol of innovation, a force to reckon,
In your presence, we find wonder awaken.

TWENTY-SEVEN

COSMIC SCHEME

In a realm where metals reign supreme,
There lies a jewel, a silvery dream.
Gallium, they call it, an element rare,
With secrets and wonders, beyond compare.
    Liquid at room temperature, it defies the norm,
A shimmering mirage, a mystical form.
Pour it in your palm, watch it dance and sway,
A molten beauty, in its fluid display.
    Gallium, the shape-shifter, a trickster in disguise,
It melts in your hands, like a lover's sighs.
Its melting point low, its spirit untamed,
A rebel element that cannot be named.
    Yet in the lab, it finds its purpose true,
A catalyst for change, in reactions it brews.

A conductor of sound, a light-bending star,
Gallium shines bright, no matter how far.
   Within its atomic structure, a story unfolds,
Of electrons and protons, tales yet untold.
A puzzle piece in the grand cosmic scheme,
Gallium, a treasure, a poet's dream.
   So let us marvel at its whimsical might,
A hidden gem, glowing in plain sight.
Gallium, the enigma, a jewel so rare,
Forever entwined in the alchemist's prayer.

TWENTY-EIGHT

MESMERIZING ELEMENT

In the depths of the periodic table's array,
Where elements dance in a cosmic ballet,
There lies an enigma, both liquid and rare,
A metal called Gallium, a gem oh so fair.

From its silvery sheen to its shimmering hue,
Gallium bewitches with a charm that is true.
With a low melting point, it defies the norm,
A captivating dance in a chemical storm.

As its atoms align, a liquid it turns,
Like molten moonlight, it gracefully churns.
A metal that's fluid, it slips through your hand,
A mesmerizing element, both strange and grand.

In laboratory glassware, it finds its home,
A catalyst for science, where wonders are known.

It merges with others, a true alchemical art,
Creating new compounds, a mystical part.

Gallium, oh Gallium, so versatile and rare,
Your presence in technology, we cannot compare.
From LEDs to semiconductors, you thrive,
A hidden force in the devices we strive.

Oh, Gallium, you embody the secrets untold,
A puzzle of nature, a tale yet unfold.
In your essence, we glimpse the wonders of creation,
A testament to science, a marvel of fascination.

TWENTY-NINE

SILENTLY PERSISTS

In the depths of the periodic table's maze,
Where elements dance in an intricate haze,
Lies a metal, not widely known,
Gallium, a beauty, to you I've shown.

A silver hue, like moonlight's gleam,
Gallium, a dream, a captivating theme,
Its melting point, a curious affair,
Just above room temperature, a rare flare.

In liquid form, it dances with grace,
A shimmering pool, a captivating embrace,
A trickster it plays, defying the norm,
Melting in your hand, a magical swarm.

Gallium, the shape-shifter, so malleable,
Bending to will, an element so pliable,

Its true form hidden, like secrets untold,
A riddle, a puzzle, a tale yet unfold.

Mysteries lie within its atomic core,
A symbol of science, forevermore,
From its discovery, a journey untamed,
Gallium, an enigma, forever unnamed.

Through the ages, it silently persists,
A silent witness, as time persists,
An element of wonders, Gallium's might,
Invisible hero, shining so bright.

So let us marvel at Gallium's grace,
A hidden gem, a treasure to embrace,
In the realm of elements, it stands apart,
Gallium, a masterpiece, etched in our heart.

THIRTY

MOONLIT WINE

In a realm of elements, a hidden gem I see,
Gallium, the mystic metal, beckons me.
Silent and serene, its secrets softly unfold,
A tale of transformation, a story yet untold.

Born in the fiery heart of the Earth's core,
Gallium emerges, a treasure to adore.
A silver shimmer, like moonlight on the sea,
Reflecting dreams of what it longs to be.

A shape-shifting sorcerer, Gallium holds the key,
To bend and mold its form, with an alchemist's decree.
With gentle warmth, it melts within my palm,
An enigma unleashed, defying all norms.

From liquid to solid, a metamorphosis profound,
Gallium dances, a mesmerizing sound.

It weaves its way through the fabric of time,
Untangling mysteries, both yours and mine.
  A catalyst of change, Gallium's true might,
Unleashes innovation, a visionary's delight.
In circuit boards, it conducts with grace,
Powering progress, in this vast technological race.
  Oh, Gallium, rare and wondrous element divine,
Your allure enchants, like moonlit wine.
In your atomic dance, I find solace and peace,
A symbol of transformation, a beauty to release.

THIRTY-ONE

LASERS AND LEDS

In the realm of elements, gallium does reside,
A metal, so unique, where wonders do hide.
With atomic number 31, it claims its name,
Gallium, the marvel, in the periodic game.

With a lustrous shine, it beckons our gaze,
A liquid at room temperature, it never betrays.
Its beauty lies in the subtlety it displays,
A chameleon of chemistry, in mysterious ways.

From its molten embrace, gallium does flow,
Like silver rivers, its currents softly glow.
It dances with magnets, a mesmerizing sight,
Defying gravity, with a touch so light.

Gallium, the magician, a master of disguise,
It infiltrates alloys with cunning and wise.

Melting points are lowered, as bonds are reformed,
Elements united, their strength transformed.

In semiconductors, gallium finds its place,
Enhancing electronics, with a steady embrace.
Lasers and LEDs, it powers their glow,
Illuminating the world, with a gallium show.

Oh, gallium, the enigma, so rare and pure,
A symbol of science, forever endure.
In laboratories and dreams, you inspire,
A testament to nature's eternal desire.

THIRTY-TWO

WHISPERS IN THE AIR

In the realm of elements, a jewel so rare,
Gallium, the metal, with secrets to share.
A shimmering beauty, elusive and bright,
A liquid at hand, but solid in sight.

Born from the earth, in nature's grand plan,
With atomic number 31, a unique brand.
Its silvery hue, like moonlight's allure,
Conceals its wonders, mystique to endure.

Gallium, the alchemist's playful friend,
With properties that twist and bend.
At room temperature, it defies the norm,
Melting in palms, like magic's warm form.

A liquid metal, so gallant and free,
It dances with ease, in liquid harmony.

A trickster it is, with a low boiling point,
A delicate dance, yet never disappoints.
  In semiconductors, it finds its true worth,
A conductor of dreams, on this spinning Earth.
It powers our gadgets, with precision and might,
Unseen by the eye, but a beacon of light.
  Gallium, a symbol of dreams unconfined,
An element of promise, a treasure to find.
Its secrets unravel, like whispers in the air,
A metal of wonder, beyond compare.

THIRTY-THREE

ENCHANTING US ALL

In the realm of elements, a marvel is found,
A metal so peculiar, it wears a crown.
Gallium, they call it, with secrets untold,
A tale of transformation, both humble and bold.

    A shimmering liquid, with silver's embrace,
It dances with heat, in a mesmerizing chase.
At room's gentle touch, it remains in repose,
But warmth is its trigger, where magic bestows.

    With joyous anticipation, it starts to melt,
The solid becomes liquid, a mesmerizing welt.
Its mercury-like form, so precious and rare,
A beauty in transition, beyond compare.

    Oh, gallant gallium, you baffle the wise,
Your low melting point, a celestial surprise.

A molten embrace, a shape-shifting role,
A metal of wonder, you truly extol.
    In laboratories, you lend your hand,
A catalyst, a helper, in reactions so grand.
From semiconductors to mirrors, you serve with pride,
An element essential in scientific stride.
    But beyond your function, lies a mystery unknown,
A symbol of adaptability, all on your own.
Gallium, you teach us, to embrace the unknown,
To transform and evolve, on paths yet unshown.
    So, let us marvel at gallium's might,
A liquid metal, so captivating and bright.
In this cosmic dance, where elements enthrall,
Gallium, you stand tall, enchanting us all.

THIRTY-FOUR

GALLIUM'S GRACE

In the realm of elements, there lies Gallium,
A liquid metal, mysterious and untamed,
A chameleon that dances with the flame,
Unveiling secrets, a seductive game.

Born from the earth, where bauxite dwells,
Extracted with precision, a story it tells,
Silvery-gray, it shimmers and gleams,
A beauty obscured, like hidden dreams.

Molten whispers caress its essence,
As it defies gravity with subtle presence,
Shape-shifting marvel, defying the norm,
A liquid metal that dares to transform.

At room's embrace, it defies the cold,
Melting away, a tale to be told,

A metal so rare, elusive and sly,
Gallium, the enigma, catches the eye.
    With mercury's kinship, it dances with glee,
A silver serpent, ever so free,
Melting in hands with a gentle touch,
A playful alchemist, it loves too much.
    Gallium, the maverick, defying the mold,
It's stories untold, yet to unfold,
A symbol of change, a symbol of might,
In this liquid metal, shines a captivating light.
    So let us marvel at Gallium's grace,
A liquid treasure in this earthly space,
For in its essence, we can perceive,
The magic of elements, where wonders cleave.

THIRTY-FIVE

INTRICATE HAND

In the realm of elements, a wonder lies,
A metal known as Gallium, a dazzling prize.
With atomic number thirty-one, it's true,
A tale of Gallium, I'll now share with you.

    A silvery shimmer upon the Earth's crust,
This element's allure we simply can't resist.
Low melting point, a curious trait,
At thirty degrees, it defies its metal state.

    Gallium, so elusive, so rare,
With secrets hidden, beyond compare.
A magician's touch, it melts in your hand,
An alchemist's dream, a marvel so grand.

    It dances with mercury, a silent tango,
A liquid embrace, a mesmerizing show.

But undeterred by its liquid form,
It transforms again, with a temperature warm.

In semiconductors, Gallium finds its place,
Powering our world, with its electrifying grace.
From LEDs to solar cells, it's a guiding light,
Harnessing its potential, shining oh-so bright.

Gallium, the element of change and surprise,
Unveiling its secrets as time flies.
A symbol of transformation, rebirth, and more,
Its uniqueness and beauty, we can't ignore.

So let us celebrate this element divine,
Gallium, a treasure, forever to shine.
In the tapestry of elements, it takes its stand,
A testament to nature's intricate hand.

THIRTY-SIX

HIDDEN GEM

In the realm of elements, a jewel unseen,
Lies a metal, gallant and serene.
Gallium, the hidden gem of the periodic table,
With properties that truly bewilder and enable.

    A silvery liquid at an ambient space,
It dances and shimmers with ethereal grace.
Beneath the surface, secrets it hides,
A metal that defies conventional tides.

    Low melting point, a mere gift of fate,
In the palm of your hand, it begins to ablate.
A touch of warmth, a gentle caress,
And gallium surrenders, without duress.

    An alchemist's dream, it transmutes with ease,
Bonding and merging as it seeks to appease.

In alloys and compounds, it finds its place,
Embarking on journeys, leaving no trace.

Yet gallium's allure extends beyond its form,
For in the heart of innovation, it takes a storm.
With gallium arsenide, it lights up the night,
Powering dreams, igniting our might.

So let us celebrate this element unseen,
A symbol of innovation, an enigma serene.
Gallium, the hidden gem of the periodic table,
Forever fascinating, its mysteries we'll enable.

ABOUT THE AUTHOR

Walter the Educator is one of the pseudonyms for Walter Anderson. Formally educated in Chemistry, Business, and Education, he is an educator, an author, a diverse entrepreneur, and he is the son of a disabled war veteran. "Walter the Educator" shares his time between educating and creating. He holds interests and owns several creative projects that entertain, enlighten, enhance, and educate, hoping to inspire and motivate you.

Follow, find new works, and stay up to date
with Walter the Educator™
at WaltertheEducator.com

www.ingramcontent.com/pod-product-compliance
Lightning Source LLC
LaVergne TN
LVHW051958060526
838201LV00059B/3713